Little Jack The Lion

A Coloring Guide For Animals

COLORCORP, INC.

4500 LEETSDALE DRIVE
DENVER, CO 80222
USA
1-800-873-7024

ISBN# 0-9651012-3-1

Printed in China

Little Jack, the Lion was spending the day with his father. His mother was away visiting *her* mother.
Jack misses his mother, even though she's not been away for long!
He decides that after his father cleans him up, he'll go find her.

Not long after he is on his way, Little Jack hears a noise in the tree
up above him. It's his neighbor the Civet.
"Jack, where are you going?" says his friend.
"To see my mother", says Jack.

Thinking only of his mother, Jack hurries on...

As he approaches the road, he sees a mongoose jumping across.

Suddenly from behind a tree, out jumps a Wolf!

"Hi there little boy..." snarls the Wolf
But Jack ignores him and moves on.......

As he travels farther down the road, Little Jack comes upon
a large female Lion sleeping in a tree.
But it's not his mother, so Jack tip-toes away,
as quietly as possible.

As Jack moves along, he day dreams about his Uncle Tiger, and how skillful of a hunter he is....

Or like his Uncle Leopard, who is so
powerful and fast.......

After awhile, he comes to a river.
But blocking the way is a huge Rhinoceros!
"How can I get across the river Mr. Rhino?" asks Little Jack.
But the Rhino just ignores him, and Jack moves along.

He sees his Cousin Cat, climbing a tree.
"How can I get across the river Cousin?" asks Little Jack.
The cat replies: "Just use your head Little Jack,
I know you'll find the answer......."

Still having no way to cross the river, Jack moves on a little farther. Then across the way, he spots his friend, Mr. Elephant.
"Hey Mr. Elephant, can you help me across the river?"
"Why sure Little Jack, what are friends for?"

Realizing he still has a long way to go, Jack asks
Mr. Horse if he can give him a ride.
"I'm sorry Little Jack, I need to rest. I've just run a long way,
and I'm all out of breath......"

So Little Jack starts off by himself. But very soon, he is
startled by the sound in the trees above him.
Looking up, he sees this ugly, angry looking animal
staring back. He decides to run.........

Jack runs as hard as he can, because he is now close to his grandmother's home. As he comes to the edge of the road, he sees an Anteater in the ditch, eating ants. "How disgusting!" Little Jack says to himself.

Little Jack is *very* close now!
He sees his Auntie Cat in the shade by the roadside.

"Auntie Cat!" shouts Little Jack.

Auntie Cat jumps up and announces Little Jack's arrival
to everyone.
"Auntie Cat..... Where's my Mother? ",
asks Little Jack.

Uncle Cat comes running over.

Little Jack says: "Uncle Cat, where's my mother?"

His other Cousin Cat comes out of the bushes and
laughs at Little Jack.
"Stop it Cousin... where's my mother?",
cries Little Jack.

Finally, Little Jack looks over the hill, and sees his mother!
"There you are mother!" shouts Little Jack.
Little Jack nuzzles up next to his mother, safe at last.
"I missed you mother", he says.
"I missed you too, my son", says his mother as she smiles at him.

Test Your Memory

1) Little Jack's friend the Civet has a very long _____?

2) The Mongoose was _____ across the road.

3) The Wolf surprises Little Jack by jumping out from behind a _____?

4) Jacks sees a female_____ sleeping in a tree.

5) Little Jacks' Uncle the Tiger is a very good:_____?

6) His Uncle Leopard is Powerful and _____?

7) The Rhinoceros was resting in the _____?

8) Little Jack's Cousin Cat told him to use his _____?

9) Finally, Jack gets across the river with the help of his friend the_____?

10) Mr. Horse can't help Little Jack, because he has just_____?

11) What is the name of the animal in the tree that scares Little Jack?_____

12) The Anteater picks up the ants off the ground with his_____?

Answers:
1) Tail 2) Jumping 3) Tree 4) Lion 5) Hunter 6) Fast
7) River 8) Head 9) Elephant 10) Run a long distance
11) A Lynx 12) Tongue